# that scares you."

For Lyndie and Asia with love and hugs—D.R.

To the fond memory of my mother-in-law, Martha Brown;
like Eleanor, a most righteous lady—G.K.

## ACKNOWLEDGMENTS

I thank the students in Stephanie Avena and Marissa Berber's third grade class
at Columbia Grammar Preparatory School in New York City for their honest
and insightful critiques of this manuscript.

—*Doreen Rappaport*

Text copyright © 2009 by Doreen Rappaport

Illustrations copyright © 2009 by Gary Kelley

This book is set in Bauer Bodoni. · First Edition · 1 3 5 7 9 10 8 6 4 2 · Printed in Singapore · Reinforced binding

Library of Congress Cataloging-in-Publication Data on file.

ISBN 978-0-7868-5141-6

Visit www.hyperionbooksforchildren.com

# ELEANOR,
## Quiet No More

### THE LIFE OF ELEANOR ROOSEVELT

WRITTEN BY **Doreen Rappaport** ⟳ ILLUSTRATED BY **Gary Kelley**

**Disney** · HYPERION BOOKS
NEW YORK

Eleanor's father adored his "Little Golden-Hair."
They talked.
She danced for him.
He hugged her and threw her into the air.
He made her feel important and loved.
But he drank a lot and wasn't home much.

Eleanor's mother thought Eleanor
was ugly and too serious.
She called her "Granny" in front of people.
Eleanor tried to please her mother by being good.
It didn't work, so she just kept quiet.

# "I wanted to sink through the floor in shame."

Eleanor's parents died before she was ten.
She and her brother went to live
with their grandmother Hall
and two aunts and two uncles
in a big, dreary house.

Her grandmother did everything
she thought was right for a little girl,
except hug and kiss her.

She hired a governess who taught Eleanor
how to cook and darn socks and towels.
A dancing teacher taught her how to waltz.
The French teacher made her memorize
parts of the Bible in French.

## "I never smiled."

When Eleanor was fifteen,
she was sent to school in England,
as girls from rich families often were then.

Her teacher, Marie Souvestre,
talked and talked about history.
She made Eleanor read all kinds of books
in many different languages.
She told Eleanor
to read and think for herself,
to find important things to do,
and to speak up for what she believed in.

She took Eleanor traveling and
let her walk about Paris by herself.
Most girls in this era were not allowed
to go out alone.
Eleanor began to feel more sure of herself
and made many friends at school.

## "She shocked me into thinking."

When Eleanor was eighteen,
she came back home.
She worked with other wealthy women
who thought it unfair that
they lived so well while
some Americans had so little.

Eleanor was shocked to see
four-year-old children
making artificial flowers
in dark, dingy apartments
in downtown New York City.
It horrified her that children
were working instead of playing.
She knew she had to help them.
She went downtown to teach.

# "Very early I knew there were men and women and children who suffered."

Sometimes Eleanor's classes met
at the same time as the parties uptown.
Grandmother was not happy.
She wanted Eleanor uptown, where
she could meet a "proper" man to marry.

Grandmother Hall should not have worried.
A rich distant cousin named
Franklin Delano Roosevelt loved Eleanor.
He thought she was smart and honest
and caring.
He loved that she listened,
for most people only pretended to.
He asked her to marry him.

She wrote to him:

## "I am so happy in your love, dearest, that all the world has changed for me."

Franklin made Eleanor happy,
but his mother, Sara, didn't.
Sara told Eleanor what clothes to buy
and what food to serve.
When Eleanor's children were born,
Sara told her how to raise them.
She built Eleanor and Franklin a house
next to hers, with connecting doors
on all floors.
She even chose their furniture.

## "I had nothing to do with it, and it is not the house I would have got. I hate it."

As unhappy as Eleanor was, she was too afraid to speak up.

In 1911, Franklin was elected
to the New York State Senate.
Eleanor packed up the family
and moved to Albany.
She liked Albany,
especially since Sara didn't live there.

Eleanor learned about government.
She listened to debates in the senate.
After she put the children to sleep,
she listened to Franklin and his friends
talk about politics.

Eleanor was a good wife for a politician.
She knew when to ask questions
and when to keep quiet.

# "It was a wife's duty to be interested in whatever interested her husband."

Two years later, Franklin got a new important job in Washington, D. C. Eleanor packed up the family again.

For four years, she was busy raising their five children
and going to fancy parties.
Then America went to war.

From early morning to midnight, Eleanor organized women
to knit warm clothes for sailors
and make coffee and sandwiches for men going off to war.

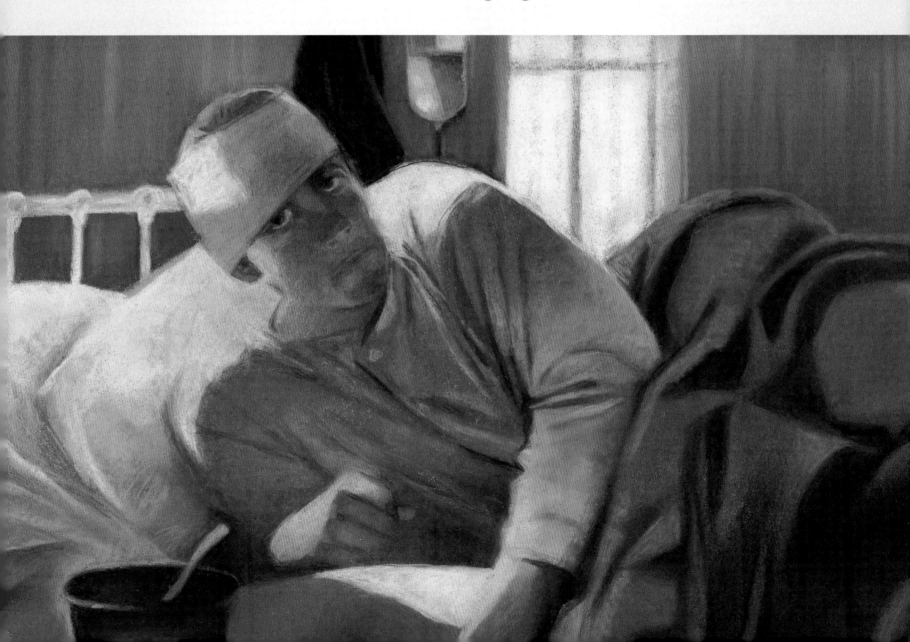

In a naval hospital, she saw men too wounded to ever go home.
Some were shell-shocked and locked behind bars.
They had no one to talk to and nothing to do all day.

Eleanor was outraged.
This time she didn't keep quiet.
She hounded public officials until these men got the best care.

# "What one has to do usually can be done."

World War I ended in 1919.
Two years later, Franklin came down
with a serious disease called polio.
The doctor said he would never walk again.

Sara said Franklin *must* stop working
and move back to the family home in Hyde Park.
Eleanor knew he dreamed of holding public office.
She had to help him realize his dream.
Sara was furious with her and
tried to turn Eleanor's children against her.
But no matter what Sara said or did,
Eleanor held firm.

# "This was the most trying winter of my life."

Franklin slowly recovered.
Meanwhile, Eleanor was very busy
caring for their five children
and teaching history and government
in a girls' school in New York City.
Her life became more separate from Franklin's.

A women's Democratic group asked her
to speak.
She worried she might not be able to
stand up, let alone talk.

# "You must do the things you cannot do."

Soon she was making more speeches
and talking on the radio and
writing magazine articles.
She reminded women,
who had recently won the vote,
that they had important things to do.

# "Women must get into politics and stay in."

In 1927, Eleanor campaigned for Franklin
when he ran for governor of New York,
urging women to vote for him.
Franklin won.
Eleanor campaigned even harder
when he ran for president in 1932.
He won that election, too.

Eleanor was now First Lady.
Hundreds of Americans wrote her
about what she *should* and *should not* do.
But Eleanor knew
she had to do and say
what she believed in.

# "Everyone must live their life in their own way."

These were hard times in America.
In this era called the Great Depression,
millions of people were out of work.
They had no money for food or housing.
Americans were scared.
Franklin sent Eleanor around the country
to talk with them.

She visited coal miners
and veterans
and sharecroppers.
No First Lady had ever done that.
She told Franklin what she saw and
what she thought needed to be done.

# "Government has a responsibility to defend the weak."

Life was especially hard for black Americans.
The South was segregated by race,
and so was Washington, D.C.
Eleanor shocked Southerners by
having a party for black girls
at the White House.

The Daughters of the American Revolution
refused to let the great black contralto
Marian Anderson sing in their auditorium.
Eleanor resigned from the group:

# "To remain a member implies approval of that action,"

she wrote in her newspaper column.
And millions read her words.

She arranged for Anderson to sing
at the Lincoln Memorial.
More than 75,000 Americans—black and white—
came to hear her.

In 1941, America was at war again.
Franklin sent Eleanor across both oceans.
She traveled thousands of miles and
met over 400,000 men and women.

She walked miles in hospital wards,
stopping at every sickbed.

"What is your name?
Is there anything
you need?
Can I take a message
home for you?"

And the military leaders,
who had not wanted her to come,
saw happiness and hope return
to the faces of their men.

All through Franklin's presidency,
Eleanor spoke up for what she believed in.
She insisted all Americans deserved
decent housing, health care, and education.

She spoke out against racism and anti-Semitism
and the internment of Japanese Americans
during World War II.

Many Americans hated what she said
and what she believed in.
They mocked her.
They called her "ugly" and "do-gooder."
But no matter what they said,
she refused to keep quiet.

"Do what you feel
in your heart to be right—
for you'll be criticized
anyway."

Franklin's health gradually weakened.
He died just at the start of his thirteenth year as president.
Eleanor was sixty years old.

# "The story is over,"

she told reporters.
But Eleanor's story wasn't over.

President Harry S. Truman appointed her
to the United Nations.
She headed a committee of people
from different countries.
Many had different ideas about
freedom and religion and human rights.

# "We must be able to disagree and to consider new ideas and not be afraid."

Eleanor listened and talked and argued.
After two years, the committee agreed
on a declaration of rights
for people all over the world:

# "All human beings are born free and equal in dignity and rights."

Eleanor was busier than ever.
When she wasn't visiting
with her grandchildren,
or writing her newspaper column,
or lecturing,
or writing her life story,
or telling politicians what to do,
she circled the globe.
She met with world leaders
and with people like you and me.

The First Lady of the United States
had become the First Lady of the World.

"We have to continue fighting
for freedom of religion,
freedom of speech,
and freedom from want."

Eleanor Roosevelt died
at the age of seventy-eight.
And the world mourned and praised
the woman who refused to be quiet.

"I have never felt that anything really mattered but knowing that you stood for the things in which you believed and had done the very best you could."

## —AUTHOR'S NOTE—

When I was a young girl, there was little information available about women and their accomplishments outside their roles of being mothers, wives, and homemakers. The one exception was Eleanor Roosevelt. In the twelve years of her husband's presidency, she became world famous, and not just because she was a "First Lady."

At that time, presidents' wives were supposed to be silent partners. She wasn't. She spoke out for what she believed in, even when it was contrary to President Roosevelt's policies.

She was a role model for me, my friends, and our mothers because she represented what was possible for women. Her courage, persistence, and determination inspired me to think about and to pursue what I believed in. I share her life with you, with the hope that you will follow her advice "Do something every day that scares you," and enjoy it.

—*Doreen Rappaport*

## —ILLUSTRATOR'S NOTE—

In this age of celebrities and politicians in the headlines for all the wrong reasons, I find Eleanor Roosevelt's story not only refreshing but essential. Like most of us, I already knew something of FDR's First Lady, but reading Doreen Rappaport's direct yet sensitive manuscript gave me much more. It made me want to do the pictures, to read between the lines and add visual information that would enhance and enlighten. I loved researching the subject almost as much as I loved making the art. The historic periods and events that shaped Eleanor and that she in turn touched are visually stimulating to me. And they make me think. Hopefully, you'll enjoy these words and pictures, and they will make you think, too.

—*Gary Kelley*

# IMPORTANT DATES

**October 11, 1884**: Anna Eleanor Roosevelt is born in New York City.

**1899–1902**: Eleanor attends Allenswood School in England.

**1903**: Eleanor teaches at Rivington Street Settlement House in New York City.

**March 17, 1905**: Eleanor marries Franklin Delano Roosevelt.

**1906**: Anna, their first child, is born.

**1907**: James is born.

**1909**: Franklin, Jr. is born, but dies in infancy from influenza.

**1910**: Elliott is born.

**1911–1913**: The family moves to Albany when Franklin is elected a New York state senator.

**1913–1920**: Franklin is Assistant Secretary of the Navy. The family lives in Washington, D.C.

**1914**: A third son, also named Franklin, Jr., is born.

**1916**: John is born.

**April 6, 1917**: The United States enters World War I. Eleanor works for the Navy Red Cross and Navy League.

**1920**: The Nineteenth Amendment passes, giving women the right to vote. Eleanor joins the League of Women Voters.

**August 1921**: Franklin contracts poliomyelitis.

**1922**: Eleanor joins the Women's Trade Union League and the Women's Division of the New York State Democratic Committee.

**1926**: With friends, Eleanor opens the Todhunter School in New York City.

**1928**: Eleanor becomes the director of the Bureau of Women's Activities of the Democratic National Committee.

**1928–1933**: Franklin is governor of New York state.

**1929**: The stock market crashes, and an economic depression sweeps through the United States.

**March 4, 1933–April 12, 1945**: Franklin serves as the thirty-second president. Eleanor is First Lady.

**1940**: Eleanor visits Great Britain as it battles to survive in World War II.

**December 7, 1941**: Pearl Harbor, in Hawaii, is bombed, and America enters World War II.

**1943**: Eleanor visits 400,000 members of the armed forces in seventeen South Pacific islands, New Zealand, and Australia.

**April 12, 1945**: Franklin Delano Roosevelt dies in Warm Springs, Georgia.

**September 2, 1945**: World War II officially ends.

**1947–1950**: Eleanor chairs the eighteen-nation United Nations Human Rights Commission.

**1954**: Eleanor supports the U.S. Supreme Court's *Brown v. Topeka Board of Education* decision.

**November 7, 1962**: Eleanor Roosevelt dies in New York City. She is buried in Hyde Park, New York, next to Franklin.

# SELECTED RESEARCH SOURCES

The Anna Eleanor Roosevelt Papers at the Franklin D. Roosevelt Presidential Library (FDRL) in Hyde Park, New York, include Eleanor Roosevelt's newspaper articles, personal correspondence, and correspondence with public officials and citizens.

Beasley, Maurine, ed., *The White House Press Conferences of Eleanor Roosevelt*. New York: Garland, 1983.

Black, Allida M., ed., *Courage in a Dangerous World: The Political Writings of Eleanor Roosevelt*. New York: Columbia University Press, 1999.

——. *What I Hope to Leave Behind: The Essential Essays of Eleanor Roosevelt*. Brooklyn, New York: Carlson Publishing, 1995.

Chadakoff, Rochelle, ed., *Eleanor Roosevelt's My Day: Her Acclaimed Columns, 1936–1945*. New York: Pharos Books, 1989.

Cook, Blanche Wiesen. *Eleanor Roosevelt: Volume One, 1884–1933*. New York: Viking Penguin, 1992.

——. *Eleanor Roosevelt: Volume Two, 1933–1938*. New York: Viking Penguin, 2000.

Goodwin, Doris Kearns. *No Ordinary Time: Franklin and Eleanor Roosevelt: The Home Front in World War II*. New York: Simon & Schuster, 1994.

Haraven, Tamara K. *An American Conscience*. New York: Quadrangle Books, 1968.

Lash, Joseph. *Eleanor and Franklin*. New York: Norton and Company, 1971.

Roosevelt, Eleanor. *The Autobiography of Eleanor Roosevelt*. New York: Harper & Row, 1958.

——. *Eleanor: The Years Alone*. New York: W. W. Norton & Company, 1972.

——. *If You Ask Me*. New York: D. Appleton-Century Company, Inc., 1946.

——. *It Seems to Me*. New York: W. W. Norton, 1954.

——. *It's Up to the Women*. New York: Frederick A. Stokes, 1933.

——. *On My Own*. New York: Harper & Brothers, 1949.

——. *This Is My Story*. New York: Harper & Brothers, 1937.

——. *Tomorrow Is Now*. New York: Harper & Row, 1963.

——. *You Learn by Living*. New York: Harper & Brothers, 1960.

If you would like to learn more about Eleanor Roosevelt and her accomplishments, read:

Adler, David A. *A Picture Book of Eleanor Roosevelt*. New York: Holiday House, 1995.

Cooney, Barbara. *Eleanor*. New York: Puffin Books, 1999.

De Young, C. Coco. *A Letter to Mrs. Roosevelt*. New York: Random House Children's Books, 2000.

Freedman, Russell. *Eleanor Roosevelt: A Life of Discovery*. Boston: Houghton Mifflin, 1997.

——. *Franklin Delano Roosevelt*. Boston: Houghton Mifflin, 1992.

Kudlinski, Kathleen. *Franklin Delano Roosevelt: Champion of Freedom*. New York: Simon & Schuster, 2003.

Kulling, Monica. *Eleanor Everywhere*. New York: Random House, 1999.

Ryan, Pam Muñoz. *Amelia and Eleanor Go for a Ride*. New York: Scholastic, 1999.

Web Sites

**National First Ladies' Library**

http://www.firstladies.org/Biographies/

**White House History**

http://www.whitehouse.gov/history/firstladies/ar32.html

**The American Experience—Eleanor Roosevelt**

http://www.pbs.org/wgbh/amex/eleanor/timeline/

# "We must cherish and honor